# BABY BLANKETS
Made with **the Knook**™

## Knooking is the new knitting!

Make 6 adorable baby blankets with the exciting new Knook! This specialized crochet hook creates true knitted fabric while the attached cord completely prevents dropped stitches! Use the Knook to make these 6 baby blankets quickly and easily. Clear instructions on the basic technique start on page 25, and are included for both right-hand & left-hand stitching, while photos illustrate each step. You'll also find excellent instruction videos at LeisureArts.com that show every stitch step-by-step. It's so much fun to fashion these sweet little blankets—because Knooking is the new knitting!

Get more! Visit LeisureArts.com for additional Knook pattern books, easy instructions, and our clear how-to videos! Look for the Knook at your local retailer or LeisureArts.com!

## TABLE OF CONTENTS

LEISURE ARTS, INC.
Little Rock, Arkansas

# BABY'S SNUGGLY THROW

**◼◼◼◻ INTERMEDIATE**

**Finished Measurement:** 35" x 42"
(89 cm x 106.5 cm)

## MATERIALS

Medium Weight Yarn
[3.5 ounces, 205 yards
(100 grams, 187 meters) per skein]:
  6 skeins
Knook, size I (5.5 mm) **or** size needed for gauge
Yarn needle

*Yarn Note:* You can use 2 colors, making 3 Panels with one color and 4 Panels with the second color. Alternate colors when joining Panels together.

**GAUGE:** Each Diamond Panel = 5" (12.75 cm) wide

**Gauge Swatch:** 5" (12.75 cm) wide
Work same as Diamond Panel, page 4, through Row 19.

**Techniques used:**
• YO *(Fig. 9, page 22)*
• K2 tog *(Figs. 10a & b, page 23)*
• Slip 1 as if to **knit**, K1, PSSO *(Fig. 11, page 23)*

## STITCH GUIDE

**RIGHT TWIST** (uses 2 sts)
Skip next st, K1 *(Fig. 1a)*, working **behind** st just made, knit the skipped st *(Fig. 1b)*.

Fig. 1a

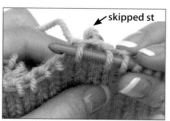

skipped st

Fig. 1b

**LEFT TWIST** (uses 2 sts)
Skip next st, K1 *(Fig. 2a)*, working in **front** of st just made, knit the skipped st *(Fig. 2b)*.

Fig. 2a

skipped st

Fig. 2b

## DIAMOND PANEL (Make 7)

Ch 23.

**Foundation Row:** Pick up 22 sts on foundation ch: 23 sts.

**Row 1** (Right side)**:** K1, work left twist, P1, K4, K2 tog, K1, (YO, K1) twice, slip 1 as if to **knit**, K1, PSSO, K4, P1, work right twist, K1.

> On the row following a yarn over, you must be careful to treat it as a stitch by purling it as instructed.

**Row 2 AND ALL WRONG SIDE ROWS:** P3, K1, P 15, K1, P3.

**Row 3:** K1, work left twist, P1, K3, K2 tog, K1, YO, K3, YO, K1, slip 1 as if to **knit**, K1, PSSO, K3, P1, work right twist, K1.

**Row 5:** K1, work left twist, P1, K2, K2 tog, K1, YO, K5, YO, K1, slip 1 as if to **knit**, K1, PSSO, K2, P1, work right twist, K1.

**Row 7:** K1, work left twist, P1, K1, K2 tog, K1, YO, K2, K2 tog, YO, K3, YO, K1, slip 1 as if to **knit**, K1, PSSO, K1, P1, work right twist, K1.

**Row 9:** K1, work left twist, P1, K2 tog, K1, YO, K2, K2 tog, YO, K1, YO, slip 1 as if to **knit**, K1, PSSO, K2, YO, K1, slip 1 as if to **knit**, K1, PSSO, P1, work right twist, K1.

**Row 11:** K1, work left twist, P1, YO, K1, slip 1 as if to **knit**, K1, PSSO, K1, K2 tog, YO, K3, YO, slip 1 as if to **knit**, K1, PSSO, K1, K2 tog, K1, YO, P1, work right twist, K1.

**Row 13:** K1, work left twist, P1, K1, YO, K1, slip 1 as if to **knit**, K1, PSSO, K7, K2 tog, K1, YO, K1, P1, work right twist, K1.

**Row 15:** K1, work left twist, P1, K2, YO, K1, slip 1 as if to **knit**, K1, PSSO, K5, K2 tog, K1, YO, K2, P1, work right twist, K1.

**Row 17:** K1, work left twist, P1, K3, YO, K1, slip 1 as if to **knit**, K1, PSSO, K3, K2 tog, K1, YO, K3, P1, work right twist, K1.

**Row 19:** K1, work left twist, P1, K4, YO, K1, slip 1 as if to **knit**, K1, PSSO, K1, K2 tog, K1, YO, K4, P1, work right twist, K1.

Repeat Rows 1-20 for pattern until Panel measure approximately 42" (106.5 cm) from foundation ch edge, ending by working Row 20.

Bind off all sts in **knit**.

## DIAMOND CHART

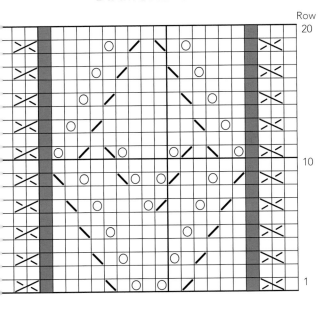

Row 20

10

1

**Note:** Follow Chart from right to left.

### KEY

☐ Knit on **right** side; purl on **wrong** side
■ Purl on **right** side, knit on **wrong** side
○ YO
☑ K2 tog
◩ Slip 1 as if to **knit**, K1, PSSO
◪ right twist
◪ left twist

## ASSEMBLY

Block each Panel *(see Blocking, page 23)*.

Sew Panels together placing foundation ch edge at the same end.

## EDGING (Make 2)

Ch 4.

**Foundation Row:** Pick up 3 sts on foundation ch: 4 sts.

**Row 1** (Right side)**:** K1, work left twist, K1.

**Row 2:** K1, P2, K1.

Repeat Rows 1 and 2 until Edging measures same width as Throw, ending by working Row 2.

Bind off all sts in pattern.

Sew an Edging to each short edge of Throw.

## EDGING CHART

Row 2
1

# MULTICOLOR CARRIAGE BLANKIE

**■□□□ BEGINNER**

**Finished Measurement:** 36" x 40"
(91.5 cm x 101.5 cm)

## MATERIALS

Medium Weight Yarn **(4)** MEDIUM
[3.5 ounces, 170 yards
(100 grams, 156 meters) per skein]:
    Color A (Cream) - 2 skeins
    Color B (Green) - 2 skeins
    Color C (Blue) - 2 skeins
    Color D (Orange) - 2 skeins
Knook, size I (5.5 mm) **or** size needed for gauge
Yarn needle
90" (228.5 cm) Cord (*see note below*)

*Note:* The blanket is worked across the width.
You will need a cord that measures approximately
twice the width plus about 18" (45.5 cm). Any thin
cord that will fit through the Knook hole may be
used.

The Garter Stitch pattern, made by knitting every
row, makes this blanket extra warm for fun carriage
rides. The 2-color look across the center of each
stripe is achieved by slipping every other stitch as
only one color is used at a time.

**GAUGE:** In pattern, 16 sts = 4" (10 cm)

**Gauge Swatch:** 4¼" (10.75 cm) wide
With Color A, ch 17.
**Foundation Row:** Pick up 16 sts on foundation ch
17 sts.
Work same as Blankie Rows 1-24, page 8.
Bind off all sts in **knit**.

Techniques used:
• Slip 1 as if to **purl** (*Fig. 7b, page 22*)

# BLANKIE

*Note:* As you work each row, slide the stitches off the Knook onto the cord when the Knook is full of stitches.

With Color A, ch 145.

**Foundation Row:** Pick up 144 sts on foundation ch: 145 sts.

**Row 1** (Right side)**:** With Color A, knit across.

**Row 2:** With Color A, knit across; drop Color A.

**Row 3:** With Color B, K1, (slip 1 as if to **purl** with yarn in **back**, K1) across.

**Row 4:** With Color B, K1, (slip 1 as if to **purl** with yarn in **front**, K1) across; cut Color B.

**Row 5:** With Color A, knit across.

**Row 6:** With Color A, knit across; cut Color A.

**Row 7:** With Color C, knit across.

**Row 8:** With Color C, knit across; drop Color C.

**Row 9:** With Color D, K1, (slip 1 as if to **purl** with yarn in **back**, K1) across.

**Row 10:** With Color D, K1, (slip 1 as if to **purl** with yarn in **front**, K1) across; cut Color D.

**Row 11:** With Color C, knit across.

**Row 12:** With Color C, knit across; cut Color C.

**Row 13:** With Color B, knit across.

**Row 14:** With Color B, knit across; drop Color B.

**Row 15:** With Color A, K1, (slip 1 as if to **purl** with yarn in **back**, K1) across.

**Row 16:** With Color A, K1, (slip 1 as if to **purl** with yarn in **front**, K1) across; cut Color A.

**Row 17:** With Color B, knit across.

**Row 18:** With Color B, knit across; cut Color B.

**Row 19:** With Color D, knit across.

**Row 20:** With Color D, knit across; drop Color D.

**Row 21:** With Color C, K1, (slip 1 as if to **purl** with yarn in **back**, K1) across.

**Row 22:** With Color C, K1, (slip 1 as if to **purl** with yarn in **front**, K1) across; cut Color C.

**Row 23:** With Color D, knit across.

**Row 24:** With Color D, knit across; cut Color D.

**Row 25:** With Color A, knit across.

Repeat Rows 2-25 for pattern until Blankie measures approximately 39³/₄" (101 cm) from foundation ch edge, ending by working Row 4.

**Last 2 Rows:** With Color A, knit across.

Bind off all sts in **knit**.

Block Blankie *(see Blocking, page 24)*.

# RIDGED PATCHWORK BLANKET

*hown on page 11.*

▢▢▢ **BEGINNER**

inished Measurement: 35" x 42"
(89 cm x 106.5 cm)

## IATERIALS
Medium Weight Yarn **④**
[5 ounces, 244 yards
(141 grams, 223 meters) per skein]:
5 skeins
Knook, size I (5.5 mm) **or** size needed for gauge
Yarn needle

his pattern is a combination of Garter Stitch
nitting right and wrong side rows) and
tockinette Stitch (knitting right side rows and
urling wrong side rows).

**GAUGE:** In pattern, 16 sts = 4" (10 cm)
Each Ridged Square = 7" (17.75 cm)

**Gauge Swatch:** 4" (10 cm) wide
Ch 16.
**Foundation Row:** Pick up 15 sts on foundation ch:
16 sts.
Work same as Ridged Square Rows 1-11.
Bind off all sts in **knit**.

## RIDGED SQUARE (Make 30)
Ch 28.

**Foundation Row:** Pick up 27 sts on foundation ch:
28 sts.

**Row 1** (Right side)**:** Knit across.

*Note:* Loop a short piece of yarn around any stitch
to mark Row 1 as **right** side and foundation ch
edge.

**Rows 2 and 3:** Knit across.

**Row 4:** Purl across.

**Rows 5-7:** Knit across.

Repeat Rows 4-7 for pattern until Square measures approximately 7" (17.75 cm) from foundation ch edge, ending by working Row 6.

Bind off all sts in **knit**.

## ASSEMBLY

Block each Square *(see Blocking, page 24)*.

Using Placement Diagram as a guide and alternating ridges with the foundation ch either at the bottom or to the right, sew Squares together forming 5 vertical strips of 6 Squares each; then sew strips together.

# MITERED EYELET BLANKET

●☐☐☐ **BEGINNER**

**Finished Measurement:** 37$\frac{1}{2}$" (95.5 cm) square

## MATERIALS
Medium Weight Yarn 
[3.5 ounces, 203 yards
(100 grams, 185 meters) per skein]:
   8 skeins
Knook, size H (5 mm) **or** size needed for gauge
Split-ring marker
Yarn needle

The Eyelet Squares are formed by beginning at one corner and working two YO's at the center of the row. The YO is a simple increase that forms the eyelets and a square at the same time.

**GAUGE:**  In Garter Stitch (knit every row),
         10 sts = 2" (5 cm)
         Each Eyelet Square = 7$\frac{1}{2}$" (19 cm)

**Gauge Swatch:** 3" (7.5 cm) square
Work same as Eyelet Square through Row 26: 29 sts.

**Techniques used:**
• YO (*Fig. 9, page 22*)

## EYELET SQUARE (Make 25)
Ch 3.

**Foundation Row:** Pick up 2 sts on foundation ch: 3 sts.

**Row 1** (Right side)**:** K1, (YO, K1) twice: 5 sts.

*Note:* Loop a short piece of yarn around any stitc to mark Row 1 as **right** side and bottom right corner.

**Row 2:** Knit across.

**Row 3:** K2, YO, K1, place a split-ring marker around stitch just made, YO, K2: 7 sts.

On the row following a yarn over, you must be careful to treat it as a stitch by knitting it as instructed.

**Row 4:** Knit across, moving split-ring marker to new st above marked st.

**Row 5:** Knit across to marked st, YO, knit marked st, move split-ring marker to stitch just made, YO, knit across: 9 sts.

Repeat Rows 4 and 5 for pattern until Square measures approximately 7$\frac{1}{2}$" (19 cm) square, ending by working Row 4.

Bind off all sts in **knit**.

## ASSEMBLY

Block each Square (*see Blocking, page 24*).

Placing all Squares in the same direction with the marked corner at the bottom right, sew Squares together forming 5 vertical strips of 5 Squares each; then sew strips together.

# HEARTS BABY BLANKET

■■■□ **INTERMEDIATE +**

**Finished Measurement:** 38" x 45½"
(96.5 cm x 115.5 cm)

## MATERIALS

Medium Weight Yarn
[6 ounces, 315 yards
(170 grams, 288 meters) per skein]:
6 skeins
Knook, size H (5 mm) **or** size needed for gauge
Yarn needle

**GAUGE:** Each Heart Square = 7½" (19 cm)

**Gauge Swatch:** 7½" (19 cm) square
Work same as Heart Square, page 16.

**Techniques used:**
- M1 (*Figs. 8a & b, page 22*)
- P2 tog (*Fig. 13, page 23*)
- P3 tog tbl (*Figs. 14a & b, page 24*)
- knit in row(s) **below** (*Figs. 15a & b, page 24*)

## STITCH GUIDE

**TWIST 2 RIGHT** (uses 3 sts)
Skip next st, K2 (*Fig. 3a*), working **behind** sts just made, knit the skipped st (*Fig. 3b*).

Fig. 3a

Fig. 3b

skipped st →

**TWIST 2 LEFT** (uses 3 sts)
Skip next 2 sts, K1 (*Fig. 4a*), working in **front** of st just made, knit the 2 skipped sts in order (*Fig. 4b*).

Fig. 4a

Fig. 4b

skipped sts

# HEART SQUARE (Make 30)

Ch 33.

**Foundation Row:** Pick up 32 sts on foundation ch: 33 sts.

**Rows 1-8:** P1, (K1, P1) across.

**Row 9** (Right side)**:** (P1, K1) 3 times, purl across to last 6 sts, (K1, P1) 3 times.

**Row 10:** P1, (K1, P1) twice, knit across to last 5 sts, P1, (K1, P1) twice.

**Rows 11-14:** Repeat Rows 9 and 10 twice.

**Row 15:** (P1, K1) 3 times, P 10, M1, [with yarn in **back**, insert knook in next st as if to **purl**, catch the yarn and pull through the st, YO, insert knook in same st from **left** to **right**, catch the yarn and pull through the st **(double increase made)**], M1, P 10, (K1, P1) 3 times: 37 sts.

**Row 16:** P1, (K1, P1) twice, K 11, P5, K 11, P1, (K1, P1) twice.

**Row 17:** (P1, K1) 3 times, P 10, K1, knit st in row **below** next st, K3, knit in st 2 rows **below** st just made, K1, P 10, (K1, P1) 3 times: 39 sts.

**Row 18:** P1, (K1, P1) twice, K 11, P7, K 11, P1, (K1, P1) twice.

**Row 19:** (P1, K1) 3 times, P 10, K1, knit in st in row **below** next st, K5, knit in st 2 rows **below** st just made, K1, P 10, (K1, P1) 3 times: 41 sts.

**Row 20:** P1, (K1, P1) twice, K 11, P9, K 11, P1, (K1, P1) twice.

**Row 21:** (P1, K1) 3 times, P9, twist 2 right, K5, twist 2 left, P9, (K1, P1) 3 times.

**Row 22:** P1, (K1, P1) twice, K 10, P 11, K 10, P1, (K1, P1) twice.

**Row 23:** (P1, K1) 3 times, P8, twist 2 right, K7, twist 2 left, P8, (K1, P1) 3 times.

**Row 24:** P1, (K1, P1) twice, K9, P 13, K9, P1, (K1, P1) twice.

**Row 25:** (P1, K1) 3 times, P7, twist 2 right, K9, twist 2 left, P7, (K1, P1) 3 times.

**Row 26:** P1, (K1, P1) twice, K8, P 15, K8, P1, (K1, P1) twice.

**Row 27:** (P1, K1) 3 times, P6, twist 2 right, K 11, twist 2 left, P6, (K1, P1) 3 times.

**Row 28:** P1, (K1, P1) twice, K7, P 17, K7, P1, (K1, P1) twice.

**Row 29:** (P1, K1) 3 times, P5, twist 2 right, K 13, twist 2 left, P5, (K1, P1) 3 times.

**Row 30:** P1, (K1, P1) twice, K6, P 19, K6, P1, (K1, P1) twice.

**Row 31:** (P1, K1) 3 times, P5, K 19, P5, (K1, P1) 3 times.

**Rows 32-34:** Repeat Rows 30 and 31 once, then repeat Row 30 once **more**.

**Row 35:** (P1, K1) 3 times, P5, K6, skip next 2 sts, , working **behind** st just made, purl the skipped sts in order, P1, skip next st, P2, working **front** of the sts just made, knit the skipped st, , P5, (K1, P1) 3 times.

**Row 36:** P1, (K1, P1) twice, K6, P7, K5, P7, K6, P1, 1, P1) twice.

**Row 37:** (P1, K1) 3 times, P5, skip next 2 sts, P1, orking in **front** of st just made, knit the 2 skipped s in order, K2, skip next st, K1, working **behind** st st made, purl the skipped st, P5, skip next st, P1, orking in **front** of st just made, knit the skipped , K2, skip next st, K2, working **behind** sts just ade, purl the skipped st, P5, (K1, P1) 3 times.

**Row 38:** P1, (K1, P1) twice, K7, P2 tog, P3 tog l and pull resulting loop through one loop on ook, K7, P2 tog, P3 tog tbl and pull resulting op through one loop on Knook, K7, P1, (K1, P1) ice: 33 sts.

**Row 39:** (P1, K1) 3 times, purl across to last 6 sts, 1, P1) 3 times.

**Row 40:** P1, (K1, P1) twice, knit across to last 5 sts, 1, (K1, P1) twice.

**Rows 41-44:** Repeat Rows 39 and 40 twice.

**Rows 45-52:** P1, (K1, P1) across.

ind off all sts in pattern.

## ASSEMBLY

Block each Square *(see Blocking, page 24)*.

Placing all Squares in the same direction, sew Squares together forming 5 vertical strips of 6 Squares each; then sew strips together.

## ATTACHED I-CORD EDGING

Ch 3.

**Foundation Row:** Pick up 2 sts on foundation ch: 3 sts.

**Row 1:** Do **not** turn, bring working yarn **behind** the 3 sts to work from **right** to **left**; K2, insert Knook in next st as if to **purl**, with **wrong** side of blanket facing, insert Knook in one st on edge, catch the yarn *(Fig. 5a)* and pull through the blanket and through one st on Knook *(Fig. 5b)*.

**Fig. 5a**

**Fig. 5b**

Repeat Row 1 around entire edge.

Do **not** turn; working from **right** to **left**, bind off all sts in **knit**; cut yarn leaving a long end for sewing.

Sew ends of I-Cord together.

# MITERED MULTICOLOR BLANKET

■■■□□ **EASY**

**Finished Measurement:** 36" x 42"
(91.5 cm x 106.5 cm)

## MATERIALS

Medium Weight Yarn 🔵**4**
[5 ounces, 256 yards
(142 grams, 234 meters) per skein]:
   Color A (Pink) - 3 skeins
   Color B (Green) - 2 skeins
   Color C (Yellow) - 1 skein
   Color D (Blue) - 1 skein
Knook, size I (5.5 mm) **or** size needed for gauge
Split-ring marker
Yarn needle

The Multicolor Squares are formed beginning by working across 2 sides and decreasing stitches at the center of the row until you reach the opposite corner, completing a square.

**GAUGE:** In Garter Stitch (knit every row),
   7 sts = 2" (5 cm)
   Each Multicolor Square = 6" (15.25 cm)

**Gauge Swatch:** 3" (7.5 cm) square
With Color D, ch 23.
**Foundation Row:** Pick up 22 sts on foundation ch: 23 sts.
**Row 1** (Right side): K 10, work double decrease, place split-ring marker around st just made, K 10: 21 sts.
**Row 2:** Knit across, moving split-ring marker to new st above marked st.
**Row 3:** Knit across to within one st of marked st, remove marker, work double decrease, place split-ring marker around st just made, knit across: 19 sts.
**Row 4:** Knit across, moving marker to new st above marked st.
**Rows 5-18:** Repeat Rows 3 and 4, 7 times: 5 sts.
**Row 19:** Remove marker, K1, work double decrease, K1: 3 sts.
**Row 20:** Slip 1 as if to **knit**, K2 tog, PSSO; cut yarn and pull end through loop on Knook.

Techniques used:
- K2 tog (*Figs. 10a & b, page 23*)
- Slip 1 as if to **knit**, K2 tog, PSSO (*Fig. 12, page 23*)

## STITCH GUIDE
### DOUBLE DECREASE (uses 3 sts)
Insert the Knook into the **front** of the second and then the first stitch on the cord as if to **knit** (*Fig. 6a*), knit next st and pull the stitch just made through both slipped sts (*Fig. 6b*).

Fig. 6a

Fig. 6b

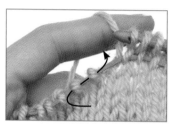

## MULTICOLOR SQUARE (Make 42)
With Color A, ch 43.

**Foundation Row:** Pick up 42 sts on foundation ch: 43 sts.

**Row 1** (Right side): K 20, work double decrease, place split-ring marker around st just made, K 20: 41 sts.

*Note:* Loop a short piece of yarn around any stitch to mark Row 1 as **right** side.

**Row 2:** Knit across, moving split-ring marker to new st above marked st.

**Row 3:** Knit across to within one st of marked st, remove marker, work double decrease, place split-ring marker around st just made, knit across: 39 sts.

**Row 4:** Knit across, moving split-ring marker to new st above marked st.

**Rows 5-10:** Repeat Rows 3 and 4, 3 times: 33 sts.

Cut Color A.

**Rows 11-20:** With Color B, repeat Rows 3 and 4, 5 times: 23 sts.

Cut Color B.

**Rows 21-30:** With Color C, repeat Rows 3 and 4, 5 times: 13 sts.

Cut Color C.

**Rows 31-38:** With Color D, repeat Rows 3 and 4, 4 times: 5 sts.

**Row 39:** Remove marker, K1, work double decrease, K1: 3 sts.

**Row 40:** Slip 1 as if to **knit**, K2 tog, PSSO; cut Color D and pull end through loop on Knook.

## ASSEMBLY
Block each Square (*see Blocking, page 24*).

Placing all Squares in the same direction with the Color D section at the top left corner and using Color A, sew Squares together forming 6 vertical strips of 7 Squares each; then sew strips together.

# GENERAL INSTRUCTIONS

## ABBREVIATIONS

| | |
|---|---|
| (s) | chain(s) |
| m | centimeters |
| | knit |
| 1 | make one |
| m | millimeters |
| | purl |
| SSO | pass slipped stitch over |
| (s) | stitch(es) |
| l | through back loop(s) |
| g | together |
| O | yarn over |

( ) or [ ] — work enclosed instructions **as many** times as specified by the number immediately following **or** work all enclosed instructions in the stitch indicated **or** contains explanatory remarks.

colon (:) — the number(s) given after a colon at the end of a row denotes the number of stitches you should have on that row.

**front** vs. **back** side — as you are working, the side facing you is the **front** of your work; the **back** is the side away from you.

**right** vs. **wrong** side — on the finished piece, the right side of your work is the side the public will see.

| Yarn Weight Symbol & Names | SUPER FINE 1 | FINE 2 | LIGHT 3 | MEDIUM 4 | BULKY 5 | SUPER BULKY 6 |
|---|---|---|---|---|---|---|
| Type of Yarns in Category | Sock, Fingering Baby | Sport, Baby | DK, Light Worsted | Worsted, Afghan, Aran | Chunky, Craft, Rug | Bulky, Roving |
| Knook Gauge Ranges in Stockinette St to 4" (10 cm) | 27-32 sts | 23-26 sts | 21-24 sts | 16-20 sts | 12-15 sts | 6-11 sts |
| Advised Knook Size Range | B-1 to D-3 | D-3 to F-5 | F-5 to G-6 | G-6 to I-9 | I-9 to K-10½ | M-13 and larger |

| KNOOK TERMINOLOGY | |
|---|---|
| **UNITED STATES** | **INTERNATIONAL** |
| gauge = | tension |
| bind off = | cast off |
| yarn over (YO) = | yarn forward (yfwd) **or** yarn around needle (yrn) |

| | | |
|---|---|---|
| ■□□□ **BEGINNER** | Projects for first-time stitchers using basic knit and purl stitches. Minimal shaping. |
| ■■□□ **EASY** | Projects using basic stitches, repetitive stitch patterns, simple color changes, knitting in the round techniques, and simple shaping and finishing. |
| ■■■□ **INTERMEDIATE** | Projects with a variety of stitches, such as basic cables and lace, simple intarsia, and mid-level shaping and finishing. |
| ■■■■ **EXPERIENCED** | Projects using advanced techniques and stitches, such as short rows, fair isle, more intricate intarsia, cables, lace patterns, and numerous color changes. |

# GAUGE

Gauge is the number of stitches and rows in every inch of your knitted piece. Exact gauge is essential for proper size. Before beginning your project, make the sample swatch given in the individual instructions in the yarn and Knook specified. After completing the swatch, measure it, counting your stitches and rows carefully. If your swatch is larger or smaller than specified, **make another, changing Knook size to get the correct gauge.** Keep trying until you find the size Knook that will give you the specified gauge.

# SLIP 1

Insert the Knook into next stitch as if you were going to **knit** *(Fig. 7a)* or as if you were going to **purl** *(Fig. 7b)* as specified in individual instructions.

Fig. 7a

Fig. 7b

# MAKE ONE *(abbreviated M1)*

Insert the Knook under the horizontal strand between the stitches from the **back** to the **front** *(Fig. 8a)*, then knit into that strand *(Fig. 8b)*.

Fig. 8a

Fig. 8b

# YARN OVER *(abbreviated YO)*

Bring the yarn to the front **under** the Knook, then back **over** the top of the Knook so that it is in position for you to knit the next stitch *(Fig. 9)*.

Fig. 9

# ECREASES

## NIT 2 TOGETHER *(abbreviated K2 tog)*

sert the Knook into the **front** of the second and
en the first stitch on the cord as if to **knit**
*ig. 10a)*, then **knit** them together as if they were
e stitch *(Fig. 10b)*.

Fig. 10a

Fig. 10b

## LIP 1, KNIT 1, PASS SLIPPED STITCH
## OVER *(abbreviated slip 1, K1, PSSO)*

lip one stitch as if to **knit** *(Fig. 7a)*. Knit the next
titch. Pull the stitch just made through the slipped
titch *(Fig. 11)*.

Fig. 11

## SLIP 1, KNIT 2 TOGETHER,
## PASS SLIPPED STITCH OVER
### *(abbreviated slip 1, K2 tog, PSSO)*

Slip one stitch as if to **knit** *(Fig. 7a)*. Knit the next
2 stitches together *(Figs. 10a & b)*. Pull the stitch
just made through the slipped stitch *(Fig. 12)*.

Fig. 12

## PURL 2 TOGETHER *(abbreviated P2 tog)*

Insert the Knook into the **front** of the first 2 stitches
on the cord as if to **purl** *(Fig. 13)*, then **purl** them
together as if they were one stitch.

Fig. 13

## PURL 3 TOGETHER THROUGH BACK LOOP (abbreviated P3 tog tbl)

Insert the Knook into the **back** loop of the first 3 stitches on the cord as if to **knit** (*Figs. 14a & b*), then **purl** them together as if they were one stitch.

Fig. 14a

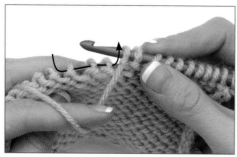

Fig. 14b

## KNIT IN ROW(S) BELOW

Insert the Knook in row **below** next stitch (*Fig. 15* **or** in stitch 2 rows **below** stitch just made (*Fig. 15* as instructed and **knit** it.

Fig. 15a

Fig. 15b

## BLOCKING

Blocking helps to smooth your work and give it a professional appearance. Check the yarn label for any special instructions about blocking.

With acrylics that can be blocked, place your project on a clean terry towel over a flat surface and pin in place to the desired size using rust-proof pins where needed. Cover it with dampene bath towels. When the towels are dry, the project is blocked.

# KNOOK BASICS

Using the Knook to create amazing knitted projects is fun and so easy! Let our step-by-step Basic Instructions show you how it's done. They're written and photographed for both left- and right-hand hooking. You'll get off to a fast start and be ready to create any of these beautiful blankets. Be sure to visit LeisureArts.com to see the video versions of these instructions—every stitch and technique in this book is there, plus a few more! You'll also find free patterns for more Knook designs!

## KNOOK PREP

Thread the cord through the hole at the end of the Knook. Gently pull the cord so that one end is approximately 8" (20.5 cm) from the Knook (*Fig. A*), leaving a long end.

Fig. A

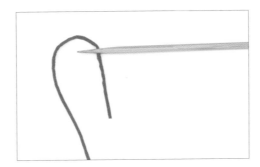

## HOLDING THE KNOOK

There are two ways to hold the Knook. Hold the Knook as you would hold a pencil (*Fig. B*), or as you would grasp a table knife (*Fig. C*). Find the manner that is most comfortable for you.

Fig. B
Right-handed

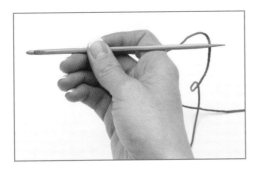

Left-handed

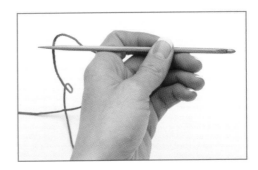

Fig. C
Right-handed

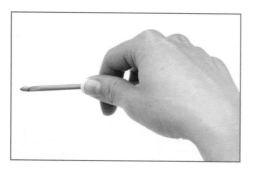

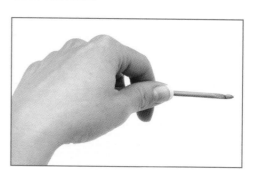

## SLIP KNOT

The first step is to make a slip knot. Pull a length of yarn from the skein and make a circle approximately 8" (20.5 cm) from the end and place it on top of the yarn. The yarn on the skein-side of the circle is the working yarn, the opposite end is the yarn tail.

Slip the Knook under the yarn in the center of the circle *(Fig. D)*, then pull on both ends to tighten *(Fig. E)*.

Fig. D
Right-handed

Left-handed

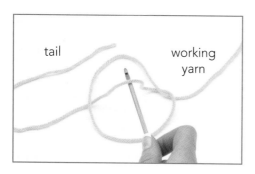

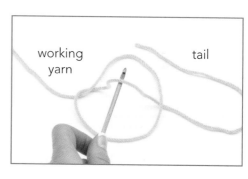

Fig. E
Right-handed

Left-handed

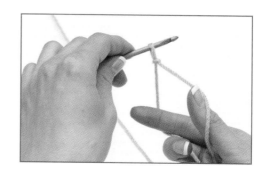

# FOUNDATION CHAIN

Once the slip knot is on the Knook, the next step is to chain the required number of stitches, which is called the foundation chain.

With the Knook in your preferred hand, hold the slip knot with your thumb and middle finger of your other hand. Loop the working yarn over your index finger, grasping it in your palm to help control the tension of your yarn as you work the stitches *(Fig. F)*.

Fig. F
Right-handed

Left-handed

Wrap the yarn around the Knook from **back** to **front** *(Fig. G)*.

Fig. G
Right-handed

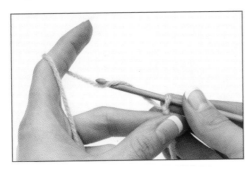

Left-handed

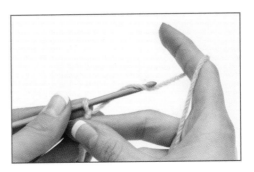

Turn the Knook to catch the yarn and draw the yarn through the slip knot *(Fig. H)*. Each time you wrap the yarn and draw the yarn through, you make one chain *(abbreviated ch)* of the foundation chain.

Fig. H
Right-handed

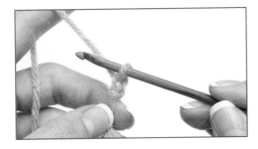

Left-handed

Repeat these steps to make the required number of chains.

If you already know how to crochet, please study the photos closely. From this point on, you will **NOT** b
using the same yarn over typically used in crochet.

## PICKING UP STITCHES

The loop on your Knook counts as the first stitch *(abbreviated st)*. To pick up the next stitch, insert the Knook from **front** to **back** into the second chain from the Knook *(Fig. I)*. With the Knook facing down, catch the yarn *(Fig. J)* and pull the yarn through the chain *(Fig. K)*.

**Fig. I**
Right-handed

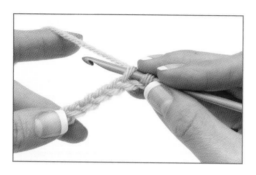

Left-handed

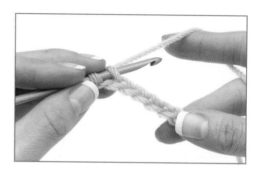

**Fig. J**
Right-handed

Left-handed

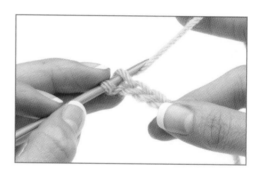

**Fig. K**
Right-handed

Left-handed

epeat until you have picked up a stitch in each chain across *(Fig. L)*.

Fig. L
Right-handed

Left-handed

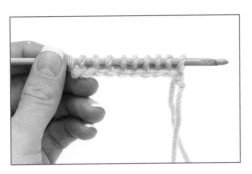

ide the stitches off the Knook onto the cord *(Fig. M)*, allowing the short end to hang freely *(Fig. N)*.

Fig. M
Right-handed

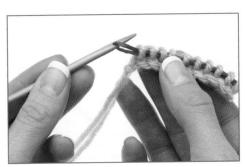

Left-handed

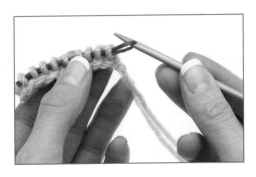

Fig. N
Right-handed

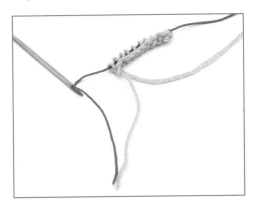

Left-handed

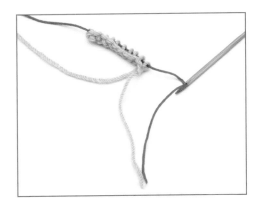

Turn your work around so that the working yarn and the yarn tail are closest to the Knook (*Fig. O*).

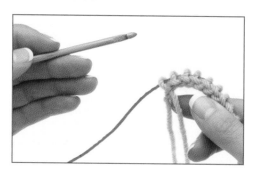

With the Knook in your preferred hand, hold your work with your other hand. Loop the working yarn over your index finger (*Fig. P*).

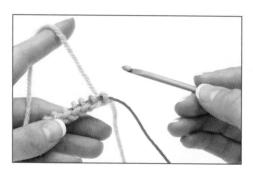

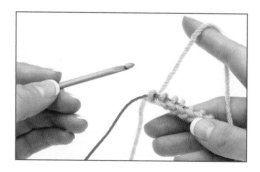

Hold the work with the yarn to the **back**.

For right-handers, insert the Knook from **left** to **right** into the first stitch *(Fig. Q)*.

Fig. Q
Right-handed

For left-handers, insert the Knook from **right** to **left** into the first stitch *(Fig. Q)*.

Fig. Q
Left-handed

With the Knook facing down, catch the yarn *(Fig. R)* and pull it through the stitch, forming a knit stitch on the Knook *(Fig. S, page 31)*.

Fig. R
Right-handed                                                    Left-handed

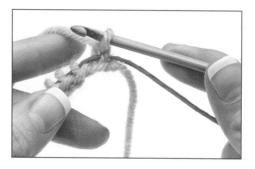
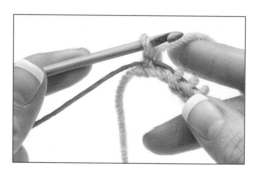

Keeping the yarn to the **back** of your work, repeat this process for each stitch across. Count the stitches to make sure you have the same number of stitches *(Fig. T)*.

Fig. T
Right-handed
Left-handed

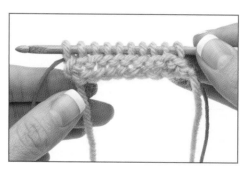

If you do not have the required number of stitches, it is very easy to fix it at this point. Simply pull the Knook back out in the opposite direction you were working until you get to the mistake, and pull the yarn to undo the stitches.

Once each stitch has been worked, gently pull the long end of the cord out of the work, leaving the new stitches on the Knook *(Fig. U)*.

Fig. U
Right-handed
Left-handed

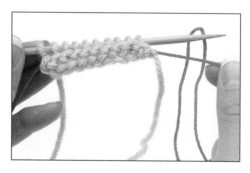
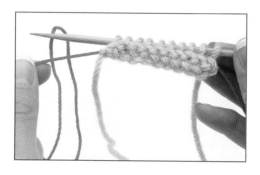

Slide the stitches off the Knook onto the long end of the cord, then turn the work.

# URL STITCH

old the work with the yarn to the **front**.

or right-handers, insert the Knook into the stitch from **right** to **left** (*Fig. V*).

Fig. V
Right-handed

or left-handers, insert the Knook into the stitch from **left** to **right** (*Fig. V*).

Fig. V
Left-handed

With the Knook facing away from you, wrap the yarn from **front** to **back** (*Fig. W*).

Fig. W
Right-handed          Left-handed

Catch the yarn with the Knook and pull the yarn through the stitch forming a purl stitch on the Knook *(Fig. X)*. Keeping the yarn to the **front** of your work, repeat this process for each stitch across the row. Once each stitch has been worked, gently pull the long end of the cord out of the work, leaving the new stitches on the Knook.

Fig. X
Right-handed

Left-handed

Slide the stitches off the Knook onto the long end of the cord, then turn the work.

Working the knit stitch on every row creates a fabric called Garter Stitch. You will also create Garter Stitch if you purl every row.

Garter Stitch

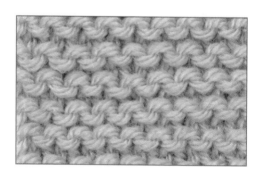

If you alternate knitting one row, then purling one row, the resulting knitted fabric is called Stockinette Stitch.

Stockinette Stitch
(right side)

Stockinette Stitch
(wrong side)

# ND OFF

nding off is the method used to remove and secure your stitches from the Knook cord so that they won't unravel.
bind off all the stitches in knit, knit the first two stitches. Pull the second stitch through the first stitch (**Fig. Y**).

**Fig. Y**
Right-handed

Left-handed

ne stitch should remain on the Knook (**Fig. Z**). Knit the next stitch and pull it through the stitch on the Knook.

**Fig. Z**
Right-handed

Left-handed

epeat this process until there are no stitches on the cord and only one stitch remains on the Knook (**Fig. AA**).

**Fig. AA**
Right-handed

Left-handed

ull the cord out of the work. Cut the yarn, leaving a long end to weave in later. Slip the remaining
titch off the Knook, pull the end through the stitch, and tighten the stitch.

o bind off in pattern, knit or purl the first two stitches as indicated for the pattern, pulling the second
titch through the first stitch as illustrated above and continuing across until all stitches are bound off.

# YARN INFORMATION

Each blanket in this leaflet was made with Medium Weight Yarn. Any brand of Medium Weight Yarn may be used. It is best to refer to the yardage/meters when determining how many balls or skeins to purchase. Remember, to arrive at the finished size, it is the GAUGE/TENSION that is important, not the brand of yarn.

For your convenience, listed below are colors used to create our photography models.

## BABY'S SNUGGLY THROW
**Patons® Canadiana**
#10615 Cherished Yellow

## MULTICOLOR CARRIAGE BLANKIE
**Lion Brand® Vanna's Choice® Baby**
Color A - #098 Lamb
Color B - #168 Mint
Color C - #106 Little Boy Blue
Color D - #132 Goldfish

## RIDGED PATCHWORK BLANKET
**Red Heart® Super Saver®**
#913 Calliope

## MITERED EYELET BLANKET
**Bernat® Baby Cakes**
#43130 Pool Party

## HEARTS BABY BLANKET
**Caron® Simply Soft®**
#9756 Lavender Blue

## MITERED MULTICOLOR BLANKET
**Red Heart® Soft Baby Steps™**
Color A - #9702 Strawberry
Color B - #9620 Baby Green
Color C - #9200 Baby Yellow
Color D - #9802 Deep Sky

We have made every effort to ensure that these instructions are accurate and complete. We cannot, however, be responsible for human error, typographical mistakes, or variations in individual work.

Production Team: Technical Writer/Editor - Cathy Hardy; Editorial Writer - Susan McManus Johnson; Senior Graphic Artist - Lora Puls; Graphic Artist - Jacob Casleton; Photo Stylist - Sondra Daniel; and Photographer - Ken West. Instructions tested and photo models made by Nancy Desmarais, Raymelle Greening, Trudy Kumpe, Dale Potter, and Margaret Taverner.